FAVORITE
Brand**Name**
RECIPES™

Dump
Soups

Make hot and hearty
soups in minutes!

pil

Publications International, Ltd.

Pictured on the front cover: Middle Eastern Chicken Soup *(page 18).*

Pictured on the back cover *(left to right):* Italian Fish Soup *(page 42)* and America's Garden Soup *(page 58).*

ISBN: 978-1-4508-9344-2

Library of Congress Control Number: 2014944049

Manufactured in China.

8 7 6 5 4 3 2 1

Microwave Cooking: Microwave ovens vary in wattage. Use the cooking times as guidelines and check for doneness before adding more time.

Preparation/Cooking Times: Preparation times are based on the approximate amount of time required to assemble the recipe before cooking, baking, chilling or serving. These times include preparation steps such as measuring, chopping and mixing. The fact that some preparations and cooking can be done simultaneously is taken into account. Preparation of optional ingredients and serving suggestions is not included.

Publications International, Ltd.

CONTENTS

SUPER SPEEDY
Chicken

Quick Hot and Sour Chicken Soup

- 2 cups water
- 2 cups chicken broth
- 1 package (about 10 ounces) refrigerated fully cooked chicken breast strips, cut into pieces
- 1 package (about 7 ounces) chicken-flavored rice and vermicelli mix
- 1 jalapeño pepper,* minced
- 2 green onions, chopped
- 1 tablespoon soy sauce
- 1 tablespoon lime juice
- 1 tablespoon minced fresh cilantro

Jalapeño peppers can sting and irritate the skin, so wear rubber gloves when handling peppers and do not touch your eyes.

1. Combine water, broth, chicken, rice mix, jalapeño, green onions and soy sauce in large saucepan; bring to a boil over high heat. Reduce heat to low; cover and simmer 20 minutes or until rice is tender, stirring occasionally.

2. Stir in lime juice; sprinkle with cilantro.

Makes 4 servings

CREAMY TUSCAN BEAN & CHICKEN SOUP

2 cans (10¾ ounces **each**) CAMPBELL'S® Condensed Cream of Celery Soup (Regular **or** 98% Fat Free)

2 cups water

1 can (about 15 ounces) white kidney beans (cannellini), rinsed and drained

1 can (about 14½ ounces) diced tomatoes, undrained

2 cups shredded **or** diced cooked chicken

¼ cup bacon bits

3 ounces fresh baby spinach leaves (about 3 cups)

Olive oil

Grated Parmesan cheese

1. Heat the soup, water, beans, tomatoes, chicken and bacon in a 3-quart saucepan over medium-high heat to a boil.

2. Stir in the spinach. Cook for 5 minutes or until the spinach is wilted. Serve the soup with a drizzle of oil and sprinkle with the cheese.

Makes 4 servings

KITCHEN TIP: For the shredded chicken, purchase a rotisserie chicken. Remove the skin and bones. You can either shred the chicken with your fingers or use 2 forks.

PREP TIME: 10 minutes
COOK TIME: 10 minutes
TOTAL TIME: 20 minutes

Chicken Tortellini Soup

6 cups chicken broth

1 package (9 ounces) refrigerated cheese and spinach tortellini

1 package (about 6 ounces) refrigerated fully cooked chicken breast strips, cut into bite-size pieces

2 cups baby spinach

4 to 6 tablespoons grated Parmesan cheese

1 tablespoon chopped fresh chives *or* 2 tablespoons sliced green onion

1. Bring broth to a boil in large saucepan over high heat. Add tortellini; cook over medium heat 5 minutes.

2. Stir in chicken and spinach; cook over low heat 3 minutes or until chicken is heated through.

3. Sprinkle with Parmesan cheese and chives.

Makes 4 servings

Spicy Thai Coconut Soup

3 cups coarsely shredded cooked chicken
(about 12 ounces)

2 cups chicken broth

1 can (15 ounces) straw mushrooms, drained

1 can (about 14 ounces) light coconut milk

1 can (about 8 ounces) baby corn, drained

1 tablespoon minced fresh ginger

½ to 1 teaspoon red curry paste

2 tablespoons lime juice

¼ cup chopped fresh cilantro

1. Combine chicken, broth, mushrooms, coconut milk, corn, ginger and red curry paste in large saucepan; bring to a simmer over medium heat. Cook until heated through.

2. Stir in lime juice; sprinkle with cilantro.

Makes 4 servings

NOTE: Red curry paste can be found in jars in the Asian aisle of large grocery stores. Spice levels can vary between brands. Start with ½ teaspoon, then add more as desired.

EASY CHICKEN, SPINACH AND WILD RICE SOUP

1 can (about 14 ounces) reduced-sodium chicken broth

1¾ cups chopped carrots

2 cans (10¾ ounces each) reduced-sodium condensed cream of chicken soup, undiluted

2 cups cooked wild rice

1 teaspoon dried thyme

¼ teaspoon dried sage

¼ teaspoon black pepper

2 cups coarsely chopped baby spinach

1½ cups chopped cooked chicken*

½ cup milk

*Half of a rotisserie chicken will yield about 1½ cups of cooked meat.

1. Bring broth to a boil in large saucepan over medium-high heat. Add carrots; cook 10 minutes.

2. Add soup, rice, thyme, sage and pepper to saucepan; bring to a boil. Stir in spinach, chicken and milk; cook and stir 2 minutes or until heated through.

Makes 6 servings

COUNTRY CHICKEN SOUP

- 5¼ cups SWANSON® Chicken Broth (Regular, Natural Goodness® **or** Certified Organic)
- ⅛ teaspoon poultry seasoning
- ⅛ teaspoon dried thyme leaves, crushed
- 1 medium carrot, sliced (about ½ cup)
- 1 stalk celery, sliced (about ½ cup)
- 1 small onion, finely chopped (about ¼ cup)
- ½ cup **uncooked** regular long-grain white rice
- 2 cans (4.5 ounces **each**) SWANSON® Premium White Chunk Chicken Breast in Water, drained

1. Heat the broth, poultry seasoning, thyme, carrot, celery and onion in a 3-quart saucepan over medium-high heat to a boil. Stir in the rice. Reduce the heat to low.

2. Cover the saucepan and cook for 20 minutes or until the rice is done.

3. Stir the chicken in the saucepan and heat through.

Makes 4 servings

PREP TIME: 10 minutes
COOK TIME: 30 minutes
TOTAL TIME: 40 minutes

CREAMY CHICKEN AND VEGGIE SOUP

2¾ cups chicken broth

2 cans (10¾ ounces each) condensed cream of chicken soup, undiluted

3 medium Yukon Gold potatoes, diced

1 cup finely chopped green onions, divided

2 cups diced cooked chicken

1 package (10 ounces) frozen peas and carrots

¼ cup half-and-half or whole milk

1. Combine broth, soup, potatoes and ½ cup green onions in large saucepan; bring to a boil over high heat. Reduce heat to low; cover and simmer 15 minutes or until potatoes are tender.

2. Stir in chicken, peas and carrots and half-and-half; cook until heated through. Sprinkle with remaining ½ cup green onions.

Makes 6 servings

Middle Eastern Chicken Soup

2½ cups water

1 can (about 14 ounces) reduced-sodium chicken broth

1 can (about 15 ounces) chickpeas, rinsed and drained

1 cup chopped cooked chicken

1 small onion, chopped

1 carrot, chopped

1 clove garlic, minced

1 teaspoon dried oregano

1 teaspoon ground cumin

½ (10-ounce) package fresh spinach, stemmed and coarsely chopped

⅛ teaspoon black pepper

1. Combine water, broth, chickpeas, chicken, onion, carrot, garlic, oregano and cumin in large saucepan; bring to a boil over high heat. Reduce heat to medium-low; cover and simmer 15 minutes.

2. Stir in spinach and pepper; simmer, uncovered, 2 minutes or until spinach is wilted.

Makes 4 servings

Asian Chicken Noodle Soup

3½ cups SWANSON® Chicken Broth (Regular, Natural Goodness® **or** Certified Organic)

1 teaspoon soy sauce

1 teaspoon ground ginger

Generous dash ground black pepper

1 medium carrot, diagonally sliced

1 stalk celery, diagonally sliced

½ red pepper, cut into 2-inch-long strips

2 green onions, diagonally sliced

1 clove garlic, minced

½ cup broken-up **uncooked** curly Asian noodles

1 cup shredded cooked chicken

1. Heat the broth, soy sauce, ginger, black pepper, carrot, celery, red pepper, green onions and garlic in a 2-quart saucepan over medium-high heat to a boil.

2. Stir the noodles and chicken in the saucepan. Reduce the heat to medium and cook for 10 minutes or until the noodles are done.

Makes 4 servings

KITCHEN TIP: For an interesting twist, use **1 cup** sliced bok choy for the celery and **2 ounces uncooked** cellophane noodles for the curly Asian noodles. Reduce the cook time to 5 minutes.

PREP TIME: 5 minutes
COOK TIME: 20 minutes
TOTAL TIME: 25 minutes

Chunky Chicken Soup

- 1 tablespoon olive oil
- 1 onion, chopped
- 1 can (about 14 ounces) diced tomatoes
- 1 cup chicken broth
- 1 cup thinly sliced carrots
- ¼ teaspoon salt
- ⅛ teaspoon black pepper
- 3 cups sliced kale or baby spinach
- 1 cup diced cooked chicken breast

1. Heat oil in large saucepan over medium-high heat. Add onion; cook and stir about 5 minutes or until golden brown. Stir in tomatoes, broth, carrots, salt and pepper; bring to a boil. Reduce heat to medium-low; simmer about 10 minutes or until carrots are tender.

2. Stir in kale and chicken; cook until kale is wilted.

Makes 2 servings

Hearty Chicken Vegetable Soup

3 cans (14 ounces **each**) SWANSON® Natural Goodness® Chicken Broth (5¼ cups)

½ teaspoon dried thyme leaves, crushed

¼ teaspoon garlic powder **or** 2 cloves garlic, minced

2 cups frozen whole kernel corn

1 package (about 10 ounces) frozen cut green beans

1 cup cut-up canned tomatoes

1 stalk celery, chopped

2 cups cubed cooked chicken **or** turkey

1. Heat the broth, thyme, garlic, corn, beans, tomatoes and celery in saucepan over medium-high heat a boil. Reduce the heat to low. Cover and cook for 5 minutes or until the vegetables are tender.

2. Stir the chicken in the saucepan and heat through.

Makes 6 servings

PREP AND COOK TIME: 25 minutes

Thai Noodle Soup

2 cans (about 14 ounces each) chicken broth

12 ounces chicken tenders, cut into ½-inch pieces

1 package (3 ounces) ramen noodles, any flavor, broken into pieces*

¼ cup shredded carrots

¼ cup frozen snow peas

2 tablespoons thinly sliced green onion

½ teaspoon minced fresh garlic

¼ teaspoon ground ginger

3 tablespoons chopped fresh cilantro

½ lime, cut into 4 wedges

Discard seasoning packet.

1. Combine broth, chicken and noodles in large saucepan; bring to a boil over medium heat. Cook 2 minutes.

2. Add carrots, snow peas, green onion, garlic and ginger. Reduce heat to low; simmer 3 minutes or until noodles are tender.

3. Sprinkle with cilantro; serve with lime wedges.

Makes 4 servings

ONE-POT
BEEF & PORK

QUICK AND ZESTY VEGETABLE SOUP

- 1 **pound lean ground beef**
- ½ **cup chopped onion**
  - **Salt and pepper**
- 2 **cans (14.5 ounces each) DEL MONTE® Italian Recipe Stewed Tomatoes**
- 2 **cans (14 ounces each) beef broth**
- 1 **can (14.5 ounces) DEL MONTE® Mixed Vegetables**
- ½ **cup uncooked medium egg noodles**
- ½ **teaspoon dried oregano**

1. Brown meat with onion in large saucepan. Cook until onion is tender; drain. Season to taste with salt and pepper.

2. Stir in remaining ingredients. Bring to boil; reduce heat.

3. Cover and simmer 15 minutes or until noodles are tender.

Makes 8 servings

PREP TIME: 5 minutes
COOK TIME: 15 minutes

KIELBASA & CABBAGE SOUP

- 1 pound Polish kielbasa, cut into ½-inch cubes
- 1 package (16 ounces) coleslaw mix (shredded green cabbage and carrots)
- 3 cans (14½ ounces each) beef broth
- 1 can (12 ounces) beer or nonalcoholic malt beverage
- 1 cup water
- ½ teaspoon caraway seeds
- 2 cups FRENCH'S® French Fried Onions, divided

  Garnish: fresh dill sprigs (optional)

1. Coat 5-quart pot or Dutch oven with nonstick cooking spray. Cook kielbasa over medium-high heat about 5 minutes or until browned. Add coleslaw mix; sauté until tender.

2. Add broth, beer, water, caraway seeds and *1 cup* French Fried Onions; bring to a boil over medium-high heat. Reduce heat to low. Simmer, uncovered, 10 minutes to blend flavors. Spoon soup into serving bowls; top with remaining onions. Garnish with fresh dill, if desired.

Makes 8 servings

PREP TIME: 10 minutes
COOK TIME: 20 minutes

QUICK AND EASY MEATBALL SOUP

    2 cans (about 14 ounces each) Italian-style stewed
       tomatoes
    2 cans (about 14 ounces each) beef broth
    1 can (about 14 ounces) mixed vegetables
    ½ cup uncooked rotini pasta or small macaroni
    ½ teaspoon dried oregano
    1 package (15 to 18 ounces) frozen Italian sausage
       meatballs without sauce, thawed according to
       package directions

1. Combine tomatoes, broth, mixed vegetables, pasta and oregano in large saucepan.

2. Stir in meatballs; bring to a boil over medium-high heat. Reduce heat to medium-low; cover and simmer 15 minutes or until pasta is tender.

Makes 4 to 6 servings

Mediterranean Bean and Sausage Soup

½ pound sweet Italian pork sausage, casings removed

1 large onion, chopped

½ teaspoon garlic powder **or** 4 cloves garlic, minced

2 cups PREGO® Traditional Italian Sauce **or** Tomato, Basil & Garlic Italian Sauce

1¾ cups SWANSON® Chicken Broth (Regular, Natural Goodness® **or** Certified Organic)

1 can (about 15 ounces) black beans **or** pinto beans

1 can (about 15 ounces) white kidney beans (cannellini), drained

1 can (about 15 ounces) red kidney beans, drained

1. Cook the sausage, onion and garlic powder in saucepan over medium-high heat until sausage is browned, stirring to separate the meat. Pour off any fat.

2. Add Italian sauce and broth and heat to a boil. Reduce the heat to low and cook for 10 minutes. Add the beans and heat through.

Makes 4 servings

PREP TIME: 10 minutes
COOK TIME: 25 minutes
TOTAL TIME: 35 minutes

Lentil Soup with Ham

3½ cups reduced-sodium chicken broth

1 pound ham slice or ham steak, trimmed and cut into bite-size pieces

1 cup dried brown lentils, rinsed and sorted

1 medium carrot, peeled and diced

½ medium onion, chopped

1 jalapeño pepper,* seeded and finely chopped

½ teaspoon dried thyme

*Jalapeño peppers can sting and irritate the skin; wear rubber gloves when handling peppers and do not touch your eyes. Wash hands after handling.

1. Combine broth, ham, lentils, carrot, onion, jalapeño and thyme in large saucepan; bring to a boil over high heat. Reduce heat to low; cover and simmer 30 minutes or until lentils are tender.

2. Let stand, covered, about 15 minutes before serving.

Makes 4 servings

COUNTRY JAPANESE NOODLE SOUP

1 can (14.5 ounces) DEL MONTE® Original Recipe Stewed Tomatoes

1 can (14 ounces) reduced sodium chicken broth

3 ounces uncooked linguine

2 teaspoons reduced-sodium soy sauce

1 to 1½ teaspoons minced gingerroot *or* ¼ teaspoon ground ginger

¼ pound sirloin steak, cut crosswise into thin strips

5 green onions, cut into thin 1-inch slivers

4 ounces firm tofu, cut into small cubes

1. Combine tomatoes, broth, pasta, soy sauce and ginger with 1¾ cups water in large saucepan; bring to boil.

2. Cook, uncovered, over medium-high heat 5 minutes.

3. Add meat, green onions and tofu; cook 4 minutes or until pasta is tender. Season to taste with pepper and additional soy sauce, if desired.

Makes 4 servings (1¼ cups each)

PREP TIME: 10 minutes
COOK TIME: 15 minutes

Pizza Meatball and Noodle Soup

1   can (about 14 ounces) beef broth

½   cup chopped onion

½   cup chopped carrot

2   ounces uncooked whole wheat spaghetti, broken
    into 2- to 3-inch pieces

1   cup zucchini slices, cut in half

8   ounces frozen fully cooked Italian-style meatballs,
    thawed

1   can (8 ounces) tomato sauce

½   cup (2 ounces) shredded mozzarella cheese

1. Combine broth, onion, carrot and pasta in large saucepan; bring to a boil over medium-high heat. Reduce heat to low; cover and simmer 3 minutes.

2. Add zucchini, meatballs and tomato sauce; return to a boil. Reduce heat to low; cover and simmer 8 minutes or until pasta is tender and meatballs are heated through, stirring occasionally.

3. Sprinkle with mozzarella.

Makes 4 servings

Sweet Potato and Ham Soup

- 1 tablespoon butter
- 1 leek, sliced
- 1 clove garlic, minced
- 4 cups reduced-sodium chicken broth
- 2 sweet potatoes, peeled and cut into ¾-inch pieces
- 8 ounces ham, cut into ½-inch pieces
- ½ teaspoon dried thyme
- 2 ounces stemmed spinach, coarsely chopped

1. Melt butter in large saucepan over medium heat. Add leek and garlic; cook and stir until tender.

2. Add broth, sweet potatoes, ham and thyme; bring to a boil over high heat. Reduce heat to low; simmer 10 minutes or until sweet potatoes are tender.

3. Stir in spinach; simmer 2 minutes or until wilted. Serve immediately.

Makes 6 servings

SEAFOOD
IN A SNAP

ITALIAN FISH SOUP

    1 cup meatless pasta sauce
    ¾ cup water
    ¾ cup reduced-sodium chicken broth
    1 teaspoon dried Italian seasoning
    ¾ cup uncooked small pasta shells
    1½ cups frozen vegetable blend, such as broccoli,
        carrots and water chestnuts or broccoli, carrots
        and cauliflower
    4 ounces fresh halibut or haddock steak, 1 inch thick,
        skinned and cut into 1-inch pieces

1. Combine pasta sauce, water, broth and Italian seasoning in medium saucepan; bring to a boil over high heat. Stir in pasta; return to a boil. Reduce heat to medium-low; cover and simmer 5 minutes.

2. Stir in frozen vegetables and fish; return to a boil. Cover and simmer over medium-low heat 4 to 5 minutes or until pasta is tender and fish flakes easily when tested with fork.

Makes 2 servings

SAVORY SEAFOOD SOUP

2½ cups water or chicken broth

1½ cups dry white wine

   1 onion, chopped

   ½ red bell pepper, chopped

   ½ green bell pepper, chopped

   1 clove garlic, minced

   ½ pound halibut, cut into 1-inch pieces

   ½ pound sea scallops, cut into halves

   1 teaspoon dried thyme

      Juice of ½ lime

      Dash hot pepper sauce

      Salt and black pepper

1. Combine water, wine, onion, bell peppers and garlic in large saucepan; bring to a boil over high heat. Reduce heat to medium-low; cover and simmer 15 minutes or until bell peppers are tender, stirring occasionally.

2. Add fish, scallops and thyme; cook 2 minutes or until fish and scallops turn opaque.

3. Stir in lime juice and hot pepper sauce; season with salt and black pepper.

Makes 4 servings

TIP: If halibut is not available, substitute cod, ocean perch or haddock.

MARYLAND-STYLE CRAB SOUP

3½ cups SWANSON® Beef Broth (Regular, 50% Less Sodium **or** Certified Organic)

1 cup CAMPBELL'S® Tomato Juice

1 tablespoon seafood seasoning

2½ cups frozen mixed vegetables

1 can (about 14½ ounces) diced tomatoes, undrained

1 medium potato, cut into ½-inch cubes (about 1 cup)

1 small onion, chopped (about ½ cup)

1 container (8 ounces) refrigerated pasteurized claw **or** lump crabmeat

Oyster crackers

1. Heat the broth, tomato juice, seasoning, mixed vegetables, tomatoes, potato and onion in a 4-quart saucepan over high heat to a boil. Reduce the heat to low. Cover and cook for 1 hour.

2. Stir in the crabmeat. Cook for 15 minutes. Serve with the crackers.

Makes 6 servings

PREP TIME: 10 minutes
COOK TIME: 1 hour 20 minutes

Gumbo in a Hurry

2 cans (14½ ounces *each*) chicken broth

1 can (14½ ounces) tomatoes, cut up, undrained

½ cup *each* minced celery and onion

¼ cup FRANK'S® REDHOT® Original Cayenne Pepper Sauce

2 bay leaves

1 teaspoon dried thyme leaves

1 pound medium raw shrimp, peeled and deveined

1 can (6 ounces) crabmeat, drained

1 (4-ounce) boneless skinless chicken breast or thigh, cut into small cubes

1 package (10 ounces) frozen sliced okra, thawed

Hot cooked rice

1. Combine broth, tomatoes, *½ cup water,* celery, onion, **Frank's RedHot** Sauce, bay leaves and thyme in large saucepan or Dutch oven. Heat to boiling. Stir in shrimp, crabmeat and chicken. Reduce heat to medium-low. Cook, uncovered, 10 minutes; stirring occasionally.

2. Stir in okra. Cook over medium-low heat 5 minutes or until okra is tender. *Do not boil.* Serve gumbo over rice in soup bowls. Serve with crusty French bread or garlic bread, if desired.

Makes 6 servings

PREP TIME: 5 minutes
COOK TIME: 15 minutes

New Orleans Fish Soup

1 can (about 15 ounces) cannellini beans, rinsed and drained

1 can (about 14 ounces) reduced-sodium chicken broth

1 yellow squash, halved lengthwise and sliced (1 cup)

1 tablespoon Cajun seasoning

2 cans (about 14 ounces each) no-salt-added stewed tomatoes

1 pound skinless firm fish fillets, such as grouper, cod or haddock, cut into 1-inch pieces

½ cup sliced green onions

1 teaspoon grated orange peel

1. Combine beans, broth, squash and Cajun seasoning in large saucepan; bring to a boil over high heat.

2. Stir in tomatoes and fish; cover and simmer over medium-low heat 3 to 5 minutes or until fish just begins to flake when tested with fork. Stir in green onions and orange peel.

Makes 4 servings

Shrimp & Corn Chowder with Sun-Dried Tomatoes

1 can (10¾ ounces) CAMPBELL'S® Condensed Cream of Potato Soup

1½ cups half-and-half

2 cups whole kernel corn, drained

2 tablespoons sun-dried tomatoes, cut into strips

1 cup small **or** medium peeled and deveined cooked shrimp

2 tablespoons chopped fresh chives

   Ground black pepper

1. Heat the soup, half-and-half, corn and tomatoes in a 3-quart saucepan over medium heat to a boil. Reduce the heat to low. Cook for 10 minutes.

2. Stir in the shrimp and chives and cook until the mixture is hot and bubbling. Season with the black pepper.

Makes 4 servings

KITCHEN TIP: For a lighter version, use skim milk instead of the half-and-half.

PREP TIME: 10 minutes
COOK TIME: 20 minutes
TOTAL TIME: 30 minutes

NO-FUSS
VEGETABLES

SALSA GAZPACHO

  1 jar (16 ounces) ORTEGA® Thick & Chunky Salsa

1½ cups water

  1 cup finely chopped celery

  1 cup diced peeled cucumber

  ½ cup finely chopped green bell pepper

  ½ cup finely chopped red bell pepper

  ¼ cup chopped green onion

  1 can (4 ounces) ORTEGA® Diced Green Chiles

  ½ teaspoon POLANER® Minced Garlic

      Salt and black pepper, to taste

  ¼ cup chopped fresh cilantro (optional)

  1 cup croutons (optional)

COMBINE salsa, water, celery, cucumber, bell peppers, green onion, chiles, garlic, and salt and pepper to taste in large bowl; mix well.

COVER and refrigerate 2 hours. If desired, top with cilantro and croutons before serving.

Makes 6 servings

Easy Mushroom Soup

1¾ cups SWANSON® 50% Less Sodium Beef Broth

1¾ cups SWANSON® Natural Goodness® Chicken Broth

⅛ teaspoon ground black pepper

⅛ teaspoon dried rosemary leaves, crushed

2 cups sliced fresh mushrooms (about 8 ounces)

¼ cup thinly sliced carrot

¼ cup finely chopped onion

¼ cup sliced celery

¼ cup fresh **or** frozen peas

1 tablespoon sliced green onion

1. Heat the beef broth, chicken broth, black pepper, rosemary, mushrooms, carrot, onion, celery and peas in a 4-quart saucepan over medium heat to a boil. Reduce the heat to low. Cover and cook for 15 minutes.

2. Add the green onion. Cook for 5 minutes or until the vegetables are tender.

Makes 4 servings

PREP TIME: 15 minutes
COOK TIME: 25 minutes
TOTAL TIME: 40 minutes

SZECHUAN VEGETABLE SOUP

2 cans (about 14 ounces each) vegetable broth

2 teaspoons minced garlic

1 teaspoon minced fresh ginger

¼ teaspoon red pepper flakes

1 package (16 ounces) frozen vegetable medley, such as broccoli, carrots, water chestnuts and red bell peppers

1 package (5 ounces) Asian curly noodles or 5 ounces uncooked angel hair pasta, broken in half

3 tablespoons soy sauce

1 tablespoon dark sesame oil

¼ cup thinly sliced green onions

1. Combine broth, garlic, ginger and red pepper flakes in large saucepan; bring to a boil over high heat. Add vegetables and noodles; cover and return to a boil. Reduce heat to medium-low; simmer, uncovered, 5 to 6 minutes or until vegetables and noodles are tender, stirring occasionally.

2. Stir in soy sauce and sesame oil; cook 3 minutes. Stir in green onions just before serving.

Makes 4 servings

NOTE: For a heartier, protein-packed main dish, add 1 package (14 ounces) extra firm tofu, drained and cut into ¾-inch cubes, to the broth mixture with the soy sauce and sesame oil.

America's Garden Soup

- 2 cans (14.5 ounces each) DEL MONTE® Diced Tomatoes with Basil, Garlic and Oregano–No Salt Added
- 2 cans (14.5 ounces each) COLLEGE INN® Light & Fat Free Chicken Broth 50% Less Sodium
- 1 can (15.25 ounces) DEL MONTE® Whole Kernel Corn–No Salt Added
- 1 can (14.5 ounces) DEL MONTE® Cut Green Beans–No Salt Added
- 1 can (14.5 ounces) DEL MONTE® Zucchini with Italian Style Tomato Sauce
- 1 can (14.5 ounces) DEL MONTE® Whole New Potatoes, cut into cubes
- 1 can (8.25 ounces) DEL MONTE® Sliced Carrots

1. Drain liquid from all vegetables, except tomatoes and zucchini.

2. Combine all ingredients in 5-quart saucepan.

3. Bring to boil. Reduce heat and simmer 3 minutes.

Makes 10 servings

Pesto and Tortellini Soup

3 cans (about 14 ounces each) chicken or vegetable broth

1 package (9 ounces) refrigerated cheese tortellini

3 to 4 cups packed stemmed fresh spinach

1 jar (7 ounces) roasted red peppers, drained and thinly sliced

¾ cup frozen green peas

1 to 2 tablespoons pesto

Grated Parmesan cheese

1. Bring broth to a boil in large saucepan over high heat. Add tortellini; return to a boil. Reduce heat to medium; simmer 6 minutes.

2. Stir in spinach, roasted peppers, peas and pesto; simmer 2 minutes or until pasta is tender.

3. Serve with Parmesan.

Makes 6 servings

PIZZA SOUP

2 cans (10¾ ounces each) condensed tomato soup

¾ teaspoon garlic powder

½ teaspoon dried oregano leaves

¾ cup uncooked tiny pasta shells (¼-inch)

1 cup shredded mozzarella cheese

1 cup FRENCH'S® French Fried Onions

1. Combine soup, *2 soup cans of water,* garlic powder and oregano in small saucepan. Bring to a boil over medium-high heat.

2. Add pasta. Cook 8 minutes or until pasta is tender.

3. Stir in cheese. Cook until cheese melts. Sprinkle with French Fried Onions.

Makes 4 servings

PREP TIME: 5 minutes
COOK TIME: 10 minutes

SOUPED-UP SOUP

  2 **cups water**

  1 **can (10¾ ounces) condensed tomato soup**

  1 **carrot, peeled and sliced**

  ¼ **cup uncooked elbow macaroni**

  ¼ **cup chopped celery**

  ¼ **cup diced zucchini**

  ½ **teaspoon dried Italian seasoning**

  ½ **cup croutons**

  2 **tablespoons grated Parmesan cheese**

1. Combine water, water, carrot, macaroni, celery, zucchini and Italian seasoning in medium saucepan; bring to a boil over medium-high heat. Reduce heat to medium-low; simmer 10 minutes or until macaroni and vegetables are tender.

2. Top with croutons and Parmesan.

Makes 4 servings

GARLIC POTATO SOUP

3½ cups **SWANSON® Chicken Broth (Regular, Natural Goodness® or Certified Organic)**

4 **cloves garlic, minced**

4 **medium red potatoes, cut into cubes (about 4 cups)**

2 **medium carrots, diced (about 1 cup)**

1 **medium onion, chopped (about ½ cup)**

1 **stalk celery, chopped (about ½ cup)**

2 **slices bacon, cooked and crumbled**

1 **cup milk**

1 **cup instant mashed potato flakes or buds**

1 **tablespoon chopped fresh parsley**

1. Heat the broth, garlic, potatoes, carrots, onion, celery and bacon in a 4-quart saucepan over medium-high heat to a boil. Reduce the heat to low. Cover and cook for 15 minutes or until the vegetables are tender.

2. Reduce the heat to medium. Stir the milk, potato flakes and parsley in the saucepan. Cook until the mixture is hot and bubbling, stirring occasionally.

Makes 4 servings

PREP TIME: 15 minutes
COOK TIME: 25 minutes
TOTAL TIME: 40 minutes

ITALIAN TOMATO AND PASTA SOUP

5 cups water

2 tablespoons dried vegetable flakes, soup greens or dehydrated vegetables

1 tablespoon minced onion

1 teaspoon sugar

1 teaspoon chicken bouillon granules

1 teaspoon dried Italian seasoning

½ teaspoon minced garlic

¼ teaspoon black pepper

1 can (about 28 ounces) crushed tomatoes

3 cups chopped fresh spinach

2½ cups uncooked farfalle (bow tie) or rotini pasta

4 to 6 slices bacon, crisp-cooked and crumbled

½ cup shredded Parmesan cheese

1. Combine water, vegetable flakes, onion, sugar, bouillon, Italian seasoning, garlic and pepper in large saucepan; bring to a boil over high heat. Boil 10 to 12 minutes.

2. Stir in tomatoes, spinach, pasta and bacon; cook over medium heat 12 to 14 minutes or until pasta is tender. Sprinkle with Parmesan.

Makes 4 to 5 servings

Spinach Tortellini Soup

4 cups SWANSON® Vegetable Broth (Regular **or** Certified Organic

¼ teaspoon garlic powder **or** 1 clove garlic, minced

¼ teaspoon black pepper

¾ cup frozen **or** shelf-stable cheese-filled tortellini (about 3 ounces)

2 cups coarsely chopped fresh spinach leaves

1. Heat the broth, garlic powder and black pepper in a 3-quart saucepan over high heat to a boil.

2. Reduce the heat to medium. Stir in the tortellini. Cook for 10 minutes. Stir in the spinach. Cook for 5 minutes or until the tortellini is tender but still firm.

Makes 6 servings

CURRIED VEGETABLE-RICE SOUP

1 package (16 ounces) frozen stir-fry vegetables

1 can (about 14 ounces) vegetable broth

¾ cup uncooked instant brown rice

2 teaspoons curry powder

½ teaspoon salt

½ teaspoon hot pepper sauce

1 can (14 ounces) unsweetened coconut milk

1 tablespoon lime juice

1. Combine vegetables and broth in large saucepan; bring to a boil over high heat. Stir in rice, curry powder, salt and hot pepper sauce; cover and simmer over medium-low heat 8 minutes or until rice is tender, stirring once.

2. Stir in coconut milk; cook 3 minutes or until heated through. Remove from heat; stir in lime juice. Serve immediately.

Makes 4 servings

TIP: To reduce fat and calories, substitute light unsweetened coconut milk for regular coconut milk.

TACO SOUP

 1 can (10¾ ounces) CAMPBELL'S® Condensed Tomato
    Soup
 1 cup milk
 2 tablespoons taco seasoning mix
 1 can (about 4 ounces) diced green chiles
18 tortilla chips, crumbled
    Shredded Monterey Jack cheese

1. Heat the soup, milk, taco seasoning and chiles in a 2-quart saucepan over medium heat for 10 minutes or until the mixture is hot and bubbling.

2. Divide the tortilla chips between **2** bowls. Pour the soup over the chips. Top with the cheese.

Makes 2 servings

PREP TIME: 5 minutes
COOK TIME: 10 minutes
TOTAL TIME: 15 minutes

QUICK
& CREAMY

SPICY PUMPKIN SOUP

1 can (15 ounces) solid-pack pumpkin

1 can (about 14 ounces) reduced-sodium vegetable or chicken broth

½ cup water

1 can (4 ounces) diced green chiles

1 teaspoon ground cumin

½ teaspoon chili powder

¼ teaspoon garlic powder

⅛ teaspoon ground red pepper (optional)

¼ cup sour cream

   Chopped fresh cilantro

1. Combine pumpkin, broth, water, chiles, cumin, chili powder, garlic powder and ground red pepper, if desired, in medium saucepan; bring to a boil over high heat. Reduce heat to medium; simmer 5 minutes, stirring occasionally.

2. Top each serving with dollops of sour cream; sprinkle with cilantro.

Makes 4 servings

Baked Potato Soup

3 cans (10¾ ounces each) condensed cream of mushroom soup

4 cups milk

3 cups diced peeled baked potatoes

½ cup cooked crumbled bacon

1 tablespoon fresh thyme leaves or 1 teaspoon dried thyme leaves

Sour cream and shredded Cheddar cheese

1½ cups FRENCH'S® French Fried Onions

1. Combine soup and milk in large saucepan until blended. Stir in potatoes, bacon and thyme. Cook over medium heat 10 to 15 minutes or until heated through, stirring frequently. Season to taste with salt and pepper.

2. Ladle soup into serving bowls. Top each serving with sour cream, cheese and 3 tablespoons French Fried Onions.

Makes 8 servings

PREP TIME: 10 minutes
COOK TIME: 15 minutes

CHEDDAR CHEESE SOUP

- ¼ cup (½ stick) butter or margarine
- ¼ cup all-purpose flour
- 2 cans (12 fluid ounces *each*) NESTLÉ® CARNATION® Evaporated Milk
- 1 cup beer or water
- 2 teaspoons Worcestershire sauce
- ½ teaspoon dry mustard (optional)
- ¼ teaspoon cayenne pepper
- 2 cups (8 ounces) shredded sharp cheddar cheese

Toppings: crumbled cooked bacon, sliced green onions, croutons

MELT butter in large saucepan. Add flour; cook, stirring constantly, until bubbly. Add evaporated milk; bring to a boil, stirring constantly. Reduce heat; stir in beer, Worcestershire sauce, mustard and cayenne pepper. Cook for 10 minutes. Remove from heat. Stir in cheese until melted. Season with salt. Serve with toppings.

Makes 4 servings

PREP TIME: 10 minutes
COOK TIME: 15 minutes

INDONESIAN CURRIED SOUP

1 can (14 ounces) coconut milk*
1 can (10¾ ounces) condensed tomato soup
¾ cup milk
3 tablespoons FRANK'S® REDHOT® Original Cayenne Pepper Sauce
1½ teaspoons curry powder

You can substitute 1 cup half-and-half for coconut milk but increase milk to 1½ cups.

1. Combine all ingredients in medium saucepan; stir until smooth.

2. Cook over low heat about 5 minutes or until heated through, stirring occasionally.

Makes 6 servings (4 cups)

PREP TIME: 5 minutes
COOK TIME: 5 minutes

CREAMY QUESO SOUP

    1 **tablespoon vegetable oil**

    1 **large onion, diced (about 1 cup)**

    1 **jar (16 ounces) PACE® Mexican Four Cheese Salsa con Queso**

    2 **cups SWANSON® Chicken Broth (Regular, Natural Goodness® or Certified Organic)**

  ¼ **cup milk**

      Crushed tortilla chips

      Chopped green onions

1. Heat the oil in a 2-quart saucepan over medium-high heat. Add the onion and cook for 10 minutes or until the onion is tender.

2. Reduce the heat to low. Stir the salsa con queso, broth and milk in the saucepan and cook for 3 minutes or until the queso mixture is hot. Serve topped with the tortilla chips and green onions.

Makes 5 servings

PREP TIME: 10 minutes
COOK TIME: 15 minutes
TOTAL TIME: 25 minutes

Pumpkin and Gorgonzola Soup

- 1 can (15 ounces) LIBBY'S® 100% Pure Pumpkin
- 1½ cups water
- 2 teaspoons MAGGI® Instant Chicken Flavor Bouillon
- 1 teaspoon ground sage
- 1 can (12 fluid ounces) NESTLÉ® CARNATION® Evaporated Milk
- ¾ cup (3 ounces) crumbled Gorgonzola cheese
- 1 large green onion, finely chopped

COOK pumpkin, water, bouillon and sage in large saucepan over medium-high heat, stirring frequently, until mixture comes to a boil.

STIR in evaporated milk and cheese. Reduce heat to low; cook, stirring frequently, until most of cheese is melted. Sprinkle with green onion before serving. Season with ground black pepper, if desired.

Makes 4 servings

PREP TIME: 10 minutes
COOK TIME: 15 minutes

HEARTY
BEANS

MINESTRONE SOUP

2 cans (about 14 ounces each) vegetable broth

1 can (28 ounces) crushed tomatoes in tomato purée

1 can (about 15 ounces) white beans, rinsed and drained

¾ cup uncooked small shell pasta

1 package (16 ounces) frozen vegetable medley, such as broccoli, green beans, carrots and red peppers

4 to 6 teaspoons pesto

1. Combine broth, tomatoes and beans in large saucepan; bring to a boil over high heat. Stir in pasta; cook 7 minutes.

2. Stir in vegetables; cook until pasta is tender and vegetables are heated through.

3. Spoon about 1 teaspoon pesto in center of each serving

Makes 4 to 6 servings

Picante Black Bean Soup

1 tablespoon reserved bacon drippings* or olive oil

1 large onion, chopped

1 clove garlic, minced

2 cans (about 15 ounces each) black beans, undrained

1 can (about 14 ounces) reduced-sodium beef broth

1¼ cups water

¾ cup picante sauce, plus additional for serving

½ teaspoon salt

½ teaspoon dried oregano

4 slices bacon, crisp-cooked and coarsely chopped*

Sour cream

*When cooking bacon, reserve drippings to use for cooking onion and garlic.

1. Heat bacon drippings in large saucepan over medium-high heat. Add onion and garlic; cook and stir 3 minutes.

2. Stir in beans with liquid, broth, water, ¾ cup picante sauce, salt and oregano. Reduce heat to low; cover and simmer 20 minutes.

3. Sprinkle with bacon; serve with sour cream and additional picante sauce.

Makes 6 to 8 servings

Quick Italian Bean, Tomato and Spinach Soup

 2 cans (about 14 ounces each) diced tomatoes with
     onions

 1 can (about 14 ounces) reduced-sodium chicken broth

 2 teaspoons sugar

 2 teaspoons dried basil

 ¾ teaspoon Worcestershire sauce

 1 can (about 15 ounces) small white beans, rinsed and
     drained

 3 ounces fresh baby spinach

 1 tablespoon extra virgin olive oil

1. Combine tomatoes, broth, sugar, basil and Worcestershire sauce in large saucepan; bring to a boil over high heat. Reduce heat to low; simmer 10 minutes.

2. Stir in beans and spinach; cook 5 minutes or until spinach is tender.

3. Stir in oil just before serving.

Makes 4 servings

Black and White Mexican Bean Soup

- 1 tablespoon vegetable oil
- 1 cup chopped onion
- ½ teaspoon POLANER® Minced Garlic
- ¼ cup all-purpose flour
- 1 packet (1.25 ounces) ORTEGA® Taco Seasoning Mix
- 2 cups milk
- 1 can (about 14 ounces) chicken broth
- 1 package (16 ounces) frozen corn
- 1 can (15 ounces) JOAN OF ARC® Great Northern Beans, rinsed, drained
- 1 can (15 ounces) ORTEGA® Black Beans, rinsed, drained
- 1 can (4 ounces) ORTEGA® Fire-Roasted Diced Green Chiles
- 2 tablespoons chopped fresh cilantro

HEAT oil in large pan or Dutch oven over medium-high heat. Add onion and garlic; cook and stir 4 to 5 minutes or until onion is tender.

STIR in flour and seasoning mix; gradually stir in milk until blended.

ADD in broth, corn, beans and green chiles; stir well. Bring to a boil, stirring constantly. Reduce heat to low; simmer 15 minutes or until thickened, stirring occasionally.

STIR in cilantro. Serve warm.

Makes 6 servings

5-Minute Heat-and-Go Soup

  1 can (about 15 ounces) navy beans, rinsed and drained

  1 can (about 14 ounces) diced tomatoes with green peppers and onions

  1 cup water

1½ teaspoons dried basil

 ½ teaspoon sugar

 ½ teaspoon chicken bouillon granules

  1 tablespoon extra virgin olive oil

1. Combine beans, tomatoes, water, basil, sugar and chicken bouillon in medium saucepan; bring to a boil over high heat. Reduce heat to low; simmer 5 minutes.

2. Remove from heat; stir in oil just before serving.

Makes 4 servings

Pasta Fagioli

1 jar (1 pound 8 ounces) RAGÚ® Chunky Pasta Sauce

1 can (19 ounces) white kidney beans, rinsed and drained

1 package (10 ounces) frozen chopped spinach, thawed

8 ounces ditalini pasta, cooked and drained (reserve
   2 cups pasta water)

1. Combine Pasta Sauce, beans, spinach, pasta and reserved pasta water in 6-quart saucepan; heat through.

2. Season, if desired, with salt, black pepper and grated Parmesan cheese.

Makes 4 servings

PREP TIME: 20 minutes
COOK TIME: 10 minutes

SLOW
COOKER SOUPS

SIMMERED SPLIT PEA SOUP

3 cans (about 14 ounces each) chicken broth

1 package (16 ounces) dried split peas, rinsed and sorted

8 slices bacon, crisp-cooked and crumbled, divided

1 onion, diced

2 carrots, diced

1 teaspoon black pepper

½ teaspoon dried thyme

1 whole bay leaf

1. Combine broth, split peas, half of bacon, onion, carrots, pepper, thyme and bay leaf in slow cooker.

2. Cover; cook on LOW 6 to 8 hours. Remove and discard bay leaf. Adjust seasonings, if desired; sprinkle with remaining bacon.

Makes 6 servings

SLOW-COOKED PANAMA PORK STEW

2 cups SWANSON® Chicken Broth (Regular, Natural Goodness® **or** Certified Organic)

4 medium sweet potatoes, peeled and cut into 2-inch pieces

2 medium green peppers, cut into 1-inch pieces (about 2 cups)

1½ cups frozen whole kernel corn, thawed

1 large onion, chopped (about 1 cup)

4 cloves garlic, minced

1 can (about 14½ ounces) diced tomatoes with green chiles

¼ cup chopped fresh cilantro leaves

1 teaspoon chili powder

2 pounds boneless pork shoulder, cut into 1-inch pieces

1. Stir the broth, sweet potatoes, peppers, corn, onion, garlic, tomatoes, cilantro, chili powder and pork in a 4½- to 5-quart slow cooker.

2. Cover and cook on LOW for 7 to 8 hours* or until the pork is fork-tender.

*Or on HIGH for 4 to 5 hours.

Makes 8 servings

PREP TIME: 20 minutes
COOK TIME: 7 to 8 hours
TOTAL TIME: 7 hours 20 minutes

TUSCAN WHITE BEAN SOUP

10 cups chicken broth

1 package (16 ounces) dried Great Northern beans,
    rinsed and sorted

1 can (about 14 ounces) diced tomatoes

1 large onion, chopped

3 carrots, chopped

6 ounces bacon, crisp-cooked and coarsely chopped

4 cloves garlic, minced

1 fresh rosemary sprig *or* 1 teaspoon dried rosemary

1 teaspoon black pepper

1. Combine broth, beans, tomatoes, onion, carrots, bacon, garlic, rosemary and pepper in slow cooker.

2. Cover; cook on LOW 8 hours. Remove and discard rosemary before serving.

Makes 8 to 10 servings

SERVING SUGGESTION: Place slices of toasted Italian bread in bottom of individual soup bowls. Drizzle with olive oil. Ladle soup over bread.

Super Easy Chicken Noodle Soup

- 1 can (about 48 ounces) chicken broth
- 2 boneless skinless chicken breasts (about 4 ounces each), cut into bite-size pieces
- 4 cups water
- ⅔ cup diced onion
- ⅔ cup diced celery
- ⅔ cup diced carrots
- ⅔ cup sliced mushrooms
- ½ cup frozen peas
- 4 chicken bouillon cubes
- 2 tablespoons butter
- 1 tablespoon dried parsley flakes
- 1 teaspoon salt
- 1 teaspoon ground cumin
- 1 teaspoon dried marjoram
- 1 teaspoon black pepper
- 2 cups cooked egg noodles

1. Combine all ingredients except noodles in slow cooker.

2. Cover; cook on LOW 5 to 7 hours or on HIGH 3 to 4 hours. Stir in noodles 30 minutes before serving.

Makes 4 servings

Leek and Potato Soup

5 cups shredded frozen hash brown potatoes

3 leeks, cut into ¾-inch pieces

1 can (10¾ ounces) condensed cream of potato soup, undiluted

1 can (about 14 ounces) reduced-sodium chicken broth

2 stalks celery, sliced

1 can (5 ounces) evaporated milk

6 slices bacon, crisp-cooked and chopped, divided

½ cup sour cream

1. Combine potatoes, leeks, soup, broth, celery, evaporated milk and all but 2 tablespoons bacon in slow cooker.

2. Cover; cook on LOW 6 to 7 hours. Stir in sour cream; sprinkle with reserved bacon.

Makes 4 to 6 servings

Lentil Soup with Beef

3 cans (10½ ounces **each**) CAMPBELL'S® Condensed French Onion Soup

1 soup can water

3 stalks celery, sliced (about 1½ cups)

3 large carrots, sliced (about 1½ cups)

1½ cups dried lentils

1 can (about 14½ ounces) diced tomatoes

1 teaspoon dried thyme leaves, crushed

3 cloves garlic, minced

2 pounds beef for stew, cut into 1-inch pieces

1. Stir the soup, water, celery, carrots, lentils, tomatoes, thyme, garlic and beef in a 5-quart slow cooker. Season as desired.

2. Cover and cook on LOW for 7 to 8 hours* or until the beef is fork-tender.

Or on HIGH for 4 to 5 hours.

Makes 8 servings

PREP TIME: 15 minutes
COOK TIME: 7 hours
TOTAL TIME: 7 hours 15 minutes

SAUSAGE AND VEGETABLE SOUP

2 cups diced potatoes

1 can (about 15 ounces) black beans, rinsed and drained

1 can (about 14 ounces) diced tomatoes

1 can (10¾ ounces) condensed cream of mushroom soup, undiluted

1 cup chopped onion

1 cup chopped red bell pepper

8 ounces turkey sausage, cut into ½-inch slices

½ cup water

2 teaspoons horseradish

2 teaspoons honey

1 teaspoon dried basil

1. Combine potatoes, beans, tomatoes, soup, onion, bell pepper, sausage, water, horseradish, honey and basil in slow cooker.

2. Cover; cook on LOW 7 to 8 hours or until potatoes are tender.

Makes 6 to 8 servings

TORTILLA SOUP

2 cans (about 14 ounces each) chicken broth

1 can (about 14 ounces) diced tomatoes with jalapeño peppers

2 cups chopped carrots

2 cups frozen corn, thawed

1½ cups chopped onions

1 can (8 ounces) tomato sauce

1 tablespoon chili powder

1 teaspoon ground cumin

¼ teaspoon garlic powder

2 cups chopped cooked chicken (optional)

Shredded Monterey Jack cheese

Crumbled tortilla chips

1. Combine broth, tomatoes, carrots, corn, onions, tomato sauce, chili powder, cumin and garlic powder in slow cooker.

2. Cover; cook on LOW 6 to 8 hours. Stir in chicken, if desired. Top with cheese and tortilla chips.

Makes 6 servings

Hearty Mushroom and Barley Soup

  9 **cups chicken broth**

  1 **package (16 ounces) sliced fresh mushrooms**

  1 **onion, chopped**

  2 **carrots, chopped**

  2 **stalks celery, chopped**

  ½ **cup uncooked pearl barley**

  ½ **ounce dried porcini mushrooms**

  3 **cloves garlic, minced**

  1 **teaspoon salt**

  ½ **teaspoon dried thyme**

  ½ **teaspoon black pepper**

1. Combine broth, sliced mushrooms, onion, carrots, celery, barley, porcini mushrooms, garlic, salt, thyme and pepper in slow cooker.

2. Cover; cook on LOW 4 to 6 hours.

Makes 8 to 10 servings

VARIATION: For even more flavor, add a beef or ham bone to the slow cooker with the rest of the ingredients.

Clam Chowder

5 cans (10¾ ounces each) condensed cream of potato soup, undiluted

2 cans (12 ounces each) evaporated skim milk

2 cans (10 ounces each) whole baby clams, rinsed and drained

1 can (about 14 ounces) cream-style corn

2 cans (4 ounces each) tiny shrimp, rinsed and drained

8 ounces bacon, crisp-cooked and crumbled

½ teaspoon lemon-pepper seasoning

Oyster crackers

1. Combine soup, milk, clams, corn, shrimp, bacon and lemon-pepper seasoning in slow cooker.

2. Cover; cook on LOW 3 to 4 hours, stirring occasionally. Serve with oyster crackers.

Makes 10 servings

BEEF FAJITA SOUP

- 1 pound beef stew meat
- 1 can (about 15 ounces) pinto beans, rinsed and drained
- 1 can (about 15 ounces) black beans, rinsed and drained
- 1 can (about 14 ounces) diced tomatoes with roasted garlic
- 1 can (about 14 ounces) beef broth
- 1½ cups water
- 1 green bell pepper, thinly sliced
- 1 red bell pepper, thinly sliced
- 1 onion, thinly sliced
- 2 teaspoons ground cumin
- 1 teaspoon seasoned salt
- 1 teaspoon black pepper

  Toppings: sour cream, shredded Monterey Jack or Cheddar cheese, chopped olives

1. Combine beef, beans, tomatoes, broth, water, bell peppers, onion, cumin, salt and black pepper in slow cooker.

2. Cover; cook on LOW 8 hours. Serve with desired toppings.

Makes 8 servings

Moroccan Chicken Soup

4 cups SWANSON® Chicken Broth (Regular, Natural Goodness® **or** Certified Organic)

3 cloves garlic, minced

2 tablespoons honey

2 teaspoons ground cumin

½ teaspoon ground cinnamon

1 can (about 14½ ounces) diced tomatoes

1 large green pepper, cut into 2-inch-long strips (about 2 cups)

1 medium onion, chopped (1 cup)

½ cup raisins

8 skinless, boneless chicken thighs (about 1 pound), cut up

Hot cooked orzo (optional)

1. Stir the broth, garlic, honey, cumin, cinnamon, tomatoes, green pepper, onion and raisins in a 3½- to 6-quart slow cooker. Add the chicken.

2. Cover and cook on LOW for 8 hours* or until the chicken is cooked through.

3. Divide the soup among **4** serving bowls. Place about ½ **cup** orzo centered on top of the soup in **each** of the serving bowls.

Or on HIGH for 4 hours.

Makes 4 servings

PREP TIME: 10 minutes
COOK TIME: 8 hours

Fiesta Black Bean Soup

     6 cups chicken broth

     1 can (about 15 ounces) black beans, rinsed and drained

    12 ounces potatoes, peeled and diced

     8 ounces diced ham

     ½ onion, diced

     1 can (4 ounces) diced green chiles

     2 cloves garlic, minced

     2 teaspoons dried oregano

    1½ teaspoons dried thyme

     1 teaspoon ground cumin

        Toppings: sour cream, chopped bell pepper and
        chopped tomatoes

1. Combine broth, beans, potatoes, ham, onion, chiles, garlic, oregano, thyme and cumin in slow cooker.

2. Cover; cook on LOW 8 to 10 hours or on HIGH 4 to 5 hours. Adjust seasonings; serve with desired toppings.

Makes 6 to 8 servings

Simple Hamburger Soup

2 pounds ground beef or turkey, cooked and drained

1 can (28 ounces) whole tomatoes, undrained

2 cans (about 14 ounces each) beef broth

1 package (10 ounces) frozen gumbo soup vegetables

½ cup uncooked pearl barley

1 teaspoon salt

1 teaspoon dried thyme

Black pepper

1. Combine ground beef, tomatoes with juice, broth, vegetables, barley, salt, thyme and pepper in slow cooker. Add water to cover.

2. Cover; cook on HIGH 3 to 4 hours or until barley and vegetables are tender.

Makes 8 servings

> TIP: Canned diced or stewed tomatoes can be substituted for the whole tomatoes. For a large crowd, add corn and serve with corn bread.

Acknowledgments

**The publisher would like to thank the companies
and organizations listed below for the use of
their recipes and photographs in this publication.**

Campbell Soup Company

Del Monte Foods

Nestlé USA

Ortega®, A Division of B&G Foods North America, Inc.

Reckitt Benckiser LLC.

Unilever

METRIC
CONVERSION CHART

VOLUME MEASUREMENTS (dry)

⅛ teaspoon = 0.5 mL
¼ teaspoon = 1 mL
½ teaspoon = 2 mL
¾ teaspoon = 4 mL
1 teaspoon = 5 mL
1 tablespoon = 15 mL
2 tablespoons = 30 mL
¼ cup = 60 mL
⅓ cup = 75 mL
½ cup = 125 mL
⅔ cup = 150 mL
¾ cup = 175 mL
1 cup = 250 mL
2 cups = 1 pint = 500 mL
3 cups = 750 mL
4 cups = 1 quart = 1 L

VOLUME MEASUREMENTS (fluid)

1 fluid ounce (2 tablespoons) = 30 mL
4 fluid ounces (½ cup) = 125 mL
8 fluid ounces (1 cup) = 250 mL
12 fluid ounces (1½ cups) = 375 mL
16 fluid ounces (2 cups) = 500 mL

WEIGHTS (mass)

½ ounce = 15 g
1 ounce = 30 g
3 ounces = 90 g
4 ounces = 120 g
8 ounces = 225 g
10 ounces = 285 g
12 ounces = 360 g
16 ounces = 1 pound = 450 g

DIMENSIONS

1/16 inch = 2 mm
⅛ inch = 3 mm
¼ inch = 6 mm
½ inch = 1.5 cm
¾ inch = 2 cm
1 inch = 2.5 cm

OVEN TEMPERATURES

250°F = 120°C
275°F = 140°C
300°F = 150°C
325°F = 160°C
350°F = 180°C
375°F = 190°C
400°F = 200°C
425°F = 220°C
450°F = 230°C

BAKING PAN SIZES

Utensil	Size in Inches/Quarts	Metric Volume	Size in Centimeters
Baking or	8×8×2	2 L	20×20×5
Cake Pan	9×9×2	2.5 L	23×23×5
(square or	12×8×2	3 L	30×20×5
rectangular)	13×9×2	3.5 L	33×23×5
Loaf Pan	8×4×3	1.5 L	20×10×7
	9×5×3	2 L	23×13×7
Round Layer	8×1½	1.2 L	20×4
Cake Pan	9×1½	1.5 L	23×4
Pie Plate	8×1¼	750 mL	20×3
	9×1¼	1 L	23×3
Baking Dish	1 quart	1 L	—
or Casserole	1½ quarts	1.5 L	—
	2 quarts	2 L	—